Pope Francis
Keys to His Thought

Copyright © 2013, Scepter Publishers, Inc.
P.O. Box 1391
New Rochelle, NY 10802
www.scepterpublishers.org

Cover and text design by Rose Design

Printed in the United States of America

ISBN: 978-1-59417-202-1

Pope Francis
Keys to His Thought

Mariano Fazio

 Scepter

From the bastion of the angels
I hear the sound of trumpets announcing
your black president
and my American Pope

———————

PERLA CASTAÑA MOLINA DE GIANELLA
EL BASTIÓN DE LOS ÁNGELES
CARDÓN, BUENOS AIRES 1983

CONTENTS

INTRODUCTION

In his address in the General Congregations before the Conclave, Cardinal Jorge Mario Bergoglio briefly sketched the need to evangelize the world—the *raison d'être* of the Church—while avoiding a self-referential and worldly attitude, and going forth to meet souls. He pointed out that it was Jesus Christ himself who prompts us from within.

> In the Book of Revelation Jesus says that he stands at the door and knocks. Obviously the text is referring to being outside the door, knocking for us to let him in. . . . But I think at times Jesus is knocking from the inside so that we might let him go out.

In the notes for his address, published with his authorization by the cardinal of Havana, Jaime Lucas Ortega, Bergoglio concluded:

> Thinking of the next Pope: . . . a man who, from contemplation of Jesus and adoration of Jesus helps the Church to go out of itself toward the existential periphery, who helps her to be

that fruitful mother who experiences the "sweet and comforting joy of evangelizing."

On March 13, 2013, following the surprising news of Benedict XVI's renunciation, and moved by the Holy Spirit, the cardinals united in Conclave elected Jorge Mario Bergoglio as the 265th successor of St. Peter, the man who in their view embodied the strongest qualifications to lead the Church to this "existential periphery." He is, in his own words "the Pope who has come from the ends of the earth," and his pastoral work in Buenos Aires, on behalf of precisely those who are considered superfluous, marginal—from a worldly point of view—is becoming better and better known.

———————— ✳ ————————

The book the reader holds in his hands was written at a time when my surprise at Cardinal Tauran's announcement of the new Pope's name was still fresh. It was written hurriedly—the date of publication is not that far removed from March 13, 2013—but seriously, and with a personal conviction of the need to make known the spiritual roots of Pope Francis. I hope to contribute with these few pages to a greater knowledge of his personality, thus helping Catholics to unite ourselves more affectively and effectively to the Roman Pontiff. May the desire of a saint of our time thus become a reality: St. Josemaría Escrivá used to say: "*Omnes cum Petro ad Iesum per Mariam*—that we might all go to Jesus, closely united to the Pope, through Mary."[1]

I have had the good fortune to be in contact with Cardinal Bergoglio with some frequency ever since the year 2000. I shared with him and other Argentinean bishops the unforgettable experience of the Fifth General Assembly of the Latin and Caribbean Bishops, which took place from May 13–31 in Aparecida, Brazil. We stayed at the same hotel, and our daily contacts helped me to deepen our acquaintanceship. Upon my return to Argentina in 2008, after an absence of twenty-seven years, we resumed frequent contact. At present I am the Regional Vicar of the Prelature of Opus Dei in Argentina and through this office our contacts intensified. I have letters of his, the memory of close and familiar telephone calls, and common concerns.

The following pages will not principally be testimonials. They are based above all on his writings and declarations. The plan is simple. In the first chapter we will cover his basic biography, from the perspective of his vocation in the Church. Afterwards we will try to describe some features of his spiritual life and continue by devoting ourselves to various manifestations of his apostolic fervor: going out in search of souls, implementing a pastoral program anchored in

---

1. St. Josemaría Escrivá, *The Forge* (New York: Scepter, 2002).

the memory of the good things that God has done for us—for humanity, for each people, for each person— dialoguing with everyone: Christians, Jews, believers in other religions, atheists, in order to reach the truth of the One who said of himself: *I am the way, the truth and the life* (Jn 14:6). The book concludes with a personal testimony and, as an appendix, an address of Cardinal Bergoglio to the priests of Buenos Aires written in 2007, in which his spiritual and apostolic dispositions are very evident.

1.

Miserando Atque Eligendo

THE VOCATION

His papal motto—*miserando atque eligendo* (freely translated as "lowly but chosen")—requires some explanation. Its significance is not as obvious as that of Benedict XVI—"Cooperators in the Truth"—nor, once the Marian context is grasped, that of Blessed John Paul II: "*Totus Tuus.*"

When I asked a compatriot what the motto meant, he replied "I believe it's a Jesuit thing." Once more I saw that most of us Argentineans are incapable of responding with a simple and humble "I don't know" to a question when we don't know the answer.

More light was provided by an article published in *L'Osservatore Romano*, signed by the theologian Inos Biffi. There it was explained that the phrase is taken from a homily of the Venerable St. Bede,

1

concerning the vocation of Matthew. We recall that the future author of the first Gospel was working as a tax collector: that is, a collaborator with the power of the imperial invader and, therefore, a sinner in the eyes of the Jews. Biffi writes:

> Bede—making repeated reference to Paul with his affirmation that Christ "has come to this world to save sinners," of which he proclaimed himself the first—insistently focuses during that Lenten homily on praise of the divine mercy, and on the "confidence of salvation" that sinners should nourish.
>
> And it is to precisely this point that the words of Pope Francis's motto refer: "Jesus saw a man called Matthew sitting at the tax office; and he said to him, 'Follow me' (Mt 9:9). He saw not only with the eyes of his body, but with those of his interior goodness. He saw a publican and, as he looked at him with merciful love in view of his choice, he said to him: 'Follow me.' He said 'Follow me,' that is, imitate me. Follow me, he said, not so much with the movement of your feet as with the practice of your life. (*L'Osservatore Romano,* Special ed., March 15, 2013)

"He looked at him with merciful love in view of his choice." This is something applicable to all souls: Our Lord chose us before the constitution of the world so "that we should be holy and blameless before him" (Eph 1:4). And he chose us knowing the clay of which we are made. But in the case of Jorge Mario Bergoglio, the phrase has a special meaning. The feast of St. Matthew is celebrated on September 21. On that date, the Liturgy of the Hours includes the homily of St. Bede that we have just cited. It was precisely on September 21—in Argentina, "Students Day"—that Bergoglio discovered his vocation of full dedication to God. He went to his parish, the Church of St. Joseph of the Flowers, one of the most traditional in the city, and decided to go to confession.

> In that confession [says the cardinal in an interview incorporated into a biography], something strange happened to me, I don't know what it was, but it changed my life; I would say that I was "caught off guard." . . . It was a surprise, the wonder of an encounter; I realized that I was being awaited. . . . From that moment on for me, God is the one who "came first."[1]

Persisting in his call to follow God, the cardinal commented on his episcopal motto:

> The religious vocation is a call of God to a soul which is expecting him consciously or unconsciously. I have always been impressed by a

---

1. S. Rubin and F. Ambrogetti, *The Jesuit: Conversations with Cardinal Jorge Bergoglio, SJ* (Buenos Aires: Vergara, 2010), p. 45 (hereafter cited as *The Jesuit*).

reading from the breviary which says that Jesus looked at Matthew with an attitude which, translated, is something like "having mercy and choosing." That was, precisely, the way in which I felt that God was looking at me during that confession. And that is the way that he has always called me to look at others: with a lot of mercy and as if I were choosing them for him: not excluding anyone, because all are chosen for the love of God. "Having mercy on him and choosing him" was the motto of my consecration as bishop and is one of the pivots of my religious experience. (*The Jesuit*, p. 49)

"You have been loved by name." The cardinal took as the basis for a retreat he preached the letters to the seven churches in the Book of Revelation. Commenting on the letter to the church of Pergamon, he referred to the passage that says the Lord will give to his chosen ones a small white stone with a new name. The cardinal preached:

The passage about the white stone with the new name, known only to God and the soul who receives it, shows a great intimacy. It happens at times that one person, inspired by love, gives to another a special name which expresses what he likes and loves in her. Certainly he does not want this name to be made public: it should remain only between him and his beloved.

The little stone has inscribed the name by which God the creator expressed the being—unrepeatable, personal, unique—of the beloved person. This is the apocalyptic intimacy, in which each member of the immense multitudes has his personal relationship with God.[2]

WORK, FAMILY, SUFFERING

The light of God which showed Bergoglio his vocation—his new name—appeared when he was seventeen. He had been born in Buenos Aires in 1936, the son of Italian immigrants from Piedmont on his father's side, and Piedmont and Liguria on his mother's.

God calls from all eternity, but the vocation becomes present at a particular place and time. Jorge Bergoglio was born in a city which at that time was one of the world's largest in population. The tango was triumphing in Paris, and Argentinean movies competed with those of Mexico throughout the Hispanic world. The Buenos Aireans had seen a lot of water flow down their Rio de la Plata since that distant 1536 when Pedro de Mendoza, of Guadix, had founded a city, or actually a village of precarious huts, destroyed by the Indians. In the year of the

---

2. Jorge Mario Bergoglio, *Mente abierta, Corazon creyente* (Buenos Aires: Claretiana, 2013), p. 154 (henceforth referred to as *Mente abierta*).

cardinal's birth, the fourth centennial of its foundation was celebrated, and a 220-foot obelisk, now one
of the symbols of the city, was unveiled. In 1580 the
city was reborn through the work of the Basque, Juan
de Garay, and it has endured to the present day. In
1620 it was the capital of a poor political territory;
being on the outskirts of the Spanish empire, it had
to live by contraband. The city prospered gradually
until it became the capital of a territory governed by
a Viceroy at the end of the eighteenth century, the
promoter of independence in 1810, and the recipient
of a growing influx of immigrants during the whole
of the nineteenth century and the early decades of
the twentieth.

In 1934, two years before Jorge's birth, an ecclesial event of the first magnitude took place in Buenos Aires: an International Eucharistic Congress.
Pope Pius XI sent Cardinal Eugenio Pacelli, Secretary
of State and the future Pope Pius XII, as papal leg-
ate. Cardinal Pacelli was surprised by the people's
response to the gathering. It was a magnificent display
of faith, marking a before and after in the history of
the Church in Argentina. On the twelfth of October,
1,200,000 people received Communion (400,000 of
them men, a remarkable fact if we take into account
the tendency in Latin American countries for there to
be a shortage of men at religious ceremonies). The
comparison with the difficult situation of Europe in
the inter-war period was obvious, and the official

addresses perhaps tended towards a certain triumphalism. But the vitality of the faith in the continent was striking, in spite of all the ideological persecutions to which the Church there had been subject for decades.

The capital of "an empire that never was," as Clemenceau defined it, presented itself to the eyes of the world as proud, cultured, and wealthy. The immigrants who abandoned Europe to reach what they considered lands of promise came chiefly from Italy and Spain, but there was no lack of French, Jews, Slavs, or those from the former Ottoman Empire. The history of the Bergoglio family was typical of millions of middle-class Argentineans. In their case, 100 percent of their blood was Italian; more common was a mixture of nationalities with an Italo-Spanish foundation.

Various financial ups and downs—so common in Argentina—required the Bergoglios to work hard to sustain themselves. They did not go hungry, but they could not afford the luxury of owning a car or going away on vacation. They were children of hard, honorable, hidden work. Jorge Mario himself had to combine his studies in secondary school, where he was preparing to be a chemical technician, with various jobs, eventually working in a laboratory.

The culture of work marked him for the rest of his life. The incessant activity of his later years was not improvised, but the fruit of well-rooted habits. He begins his day very early, at four in the morning, and usually sleeps for only five hours. His punctuality

was proverbial in Buenos Aires: he used to arrive well
in advance of the time set for liturgical ceremonies or
wherever his pastoral activity was required. He had
a sustained rhythm of work, but without giving the
impression of haste. The cardinal always found time
to dedicate to others in spite of his multiple commit-
ments, personal or telephonic, and his answering of
innumerable letters, always writing his replies in his
own hand, placing them in the envelope, and addressing them personally.

His personal experience of the world of work—
like that of John Paul II—made it easy for him to
understand the manual laborers and other workers in
their joys and sorrows. And it led him to champion
the recovery of a culture of work in an Argentina
that in recent years had fallen into the anticulture of
welfarism. He considered work the key point of the
modern social doctrine of the Church. Every year on
August 7, he celebrated Holy Mass at the Shrine of
St. Cajetan, one of the country's most popular saints
and the patron of the unemployed and job-seekers.
Millions of people go to St. Cajetan asking for food
and work, and the cardinal always accompanied them
in their prayers.

These life circumstances helped Jorge Bergoglio
to develop one of the most marked characteristics of
his personality: his austerity, evident in his modest
needs, his use of public transport, and his detachment
from material goods.

His initiation into the world of work arose through the needs of his family. The Bergoglio Sivori family was composed of his parents, his grandparents, and five brothers and sisters of whom Jorge was the oldest. They were practicing Catholics who formed a normal middle-class family in a neighborhood of populous Buenos Aires. Here he learned the family virtues of respect and affection for parents, hearty fraternity, and mutual help. He was also given a taste for culture. His mother had her children listen to the opera programs broadcast by the National Radio, explaining the plots and telling them when the most important scenes were coming. As a good Buenos Airean, he also learned from his father to follow a soccer team—in his case San Lorenzo de Almagro's—and to actively take part in sports.

It was a healthy family environment: a culture of work and honest recreation. Suffering also touched them. I recall one day when I was walking with the cardinal from the hotel at the Shrine of Aparecida, a few hundred yards. It was hot, and the cardinal was rather heavily dressed. When I asked him if he didn't feel warm, he told me that he was missing half a lung and so had to be careful. Later I learned that when he was twenty-one he had a very serious lung infection, which forced the doctors to remove the upper part of his right lung. The youth suffered a lot and none of the consolation he received from his relatives and friends helped very much until a nun told him that with his suffering he was imitating Jesus in his Passion. This supernatural reasoning was what really gave meaning to this very painful episode, and he came to see the sufferings of human life from this Christ-centered viewpoint.

From Novice to Cardinal of Buenos Aires

But let's return to his vocation. After that confession on September 21, three years passed before he entered the seminary of Buenos Aires, later to opt for the Jesuit novitiate, which he entered on March 11, 1958. What attracted him to the Society of Jesus was its emphasis on apostolic mission. He expressed to his superiors his desire to be sent to Japan but was refused because of his imperfect health.

As part of his Jesuit formation he studied liberal arts in Chile, and in 1960, back in Buenos Aires, he received his licentiate in philosophy in the Colegio Máximo San José in San Miguel, a town in the outlying suburbs of Buenos Aires. In 1964 and 1965 he was professor of literature and psychology at Immaculada High School of Santa Fe. The following year he taught the same subjects at Salvador High School in Buenos Aires. His time of teaching literature left its mark. He is a tireless reader and frequently cites literary works in his homilies and writings. The current president of Argentina's bishops conference, José

María Arancedo, recalls asking the cardinal where he had spent his vacation. He said he had stayed where he was, praying and reading (or re-reading) the classics.

> His answer surprised me, but it was useful to me and I have tried to put it into practice. How much we have lost by the rupture with the classics. This . . . explains his good use of language and the beauty of his writing. (*Mente abierta*, Prologue, p. 6)

In 1970 he received his licentiate in theology in the Colegio Máximo of St. Michael. Earlier, on December 13, 1969, he had been ordained a priest. In 1971 he made his Tertianship in Alcala de Henares, and on April 22, 1973, his perpetual profession. After serving as novice master in 1972 and 1973, he was elected Jesuit provincial of Argentina, a position he held for six years. Following a period in Germany, working on a doctoral thesis on Romano Guardini, he carried out his work in the Colegio del Salvador in Buenos Aires, and in the Jesuit church in Córdoba, as confessor and spiritual director. Between 1980 and 1986 he was rector of the Colegio Máximo.

In 1992 he was named Auxiliary Bishop of Buenos Aires by Blessed John Paul II. In 1997 he became Coadjutor Archbishop with right of succession to Cardinal Quarracino, at whose death he succeeded him as Archbishop of Buenos Aires. In 2001, John

Paul II made him a cardinal. He also served two terms as president of the Argentinean bishops conference.

It would take too long to detail the fluctuations of fortune that Argentina endured during the years Bergoglio occupied so many positions of responsibility. The political instability after 1955, following the overthrow of Juan Perón, whose political party was outlawed; the violence unleashed by the military coup and the growth of military repression, with its aftermath of deaths, disappearances of persons, and wounds inflicted on the social fabric that are still unhealed; the recurrent economic crises, especially that of 2001, which reached unimagined dimensions: this was the framework within which his pastoral activity unfolded.

The unjust accusations that arose around the disappearance of two priests while he was the Jesuit provincial were proved untrue by more accurate information showing that thanks to his intervention many lives were saved during the blackest years of recent Argentinean history. A firm defender of the dignity of the human person in all its dimensions, a lover of dialogue and of social peace, Jorge Bergoglio was a moral reference point for millions of Argentineans in recent decades.

2.

From the Contemplation of Jesus Christ

THE PERSPECTIVE OF FAITH

Meeting with journalists a few days after his election to the See of Peter, Pope Francis thanked them for the great work they had carried out in these circumstances. He added that he was especially grateful for those who had communicated the news from the perspective of faith:

> Ecclesial events are certainly no more intricate than political or economic ones! But they do have one particular underlying feature: they follow a pattern which does not readily correspond to the "worldly" categories which we are accustomed to use, and so it is not easy to interpret and communicate them to a wider and

more varied audience. The Church is certainly
a human and historical institution . . . yet her
nature is not essentially political but spiritual.

He also recalled—as had Benedict XVI—that it is
Christ who governs the Church. Its center is Christ.
In him are found truth, beauty, and goodness. The
only thing that can satisfy the human person's yearn-
ing for transcendence, he insisted to the cardinals, is
the Lord.

In his early addresses he warned against the temptation of confusing the Church with an NGO; at the
same time, he recalled that the Church is bathed in
Christ's blood, shed on the Cross. He had no hesita-
tion about citing Léon Bloy, a "politically incorrect"
thinker, who affirmed that those who do not pray to
God are praying to the devil.

These brief references to his initial discourses give
us the key to understanding the spiritual attitude of
Jorge Bergoglio. His continual denunciations in Buenos Aires of corruption, exploitation of the poorest,
human trafficking, drugs, and unemployment cannot
be read solely through the lens of a merely human
social concern. This would be to convert the cardinal
into a loudspeaker for a social-services NGO. All of
his concern for the marginalized came from his personal encounter with Christ, developed through a
life of prayer that drew the consequences of pastoral
charity from contemplation.

CHRIST-CENTERED SPIRITUAL LIFE IN THE CHURCH

It is very difficult to describe in just a few pages the outstanding features of someone's spiritual life as manifest in his words and actions. Moreover, at the core of the human soul is a mystery known to God alone. But this is no obstacle to trying to delineate some features. I have structured what follows in this way—there are many other possibilities—starting from his certainty of God's call, which confers a mission upon each one of us. Every Christian vocation is a definite invitation to identify oneself with Christ, and Christ crucified. Following Christ implies belonging to the Church, which guards the faith, a faith we have to ask for, and which grows in a life of continuous prayer. We will see these features exemplified with texts from Cardinal Bergoglio.

In the previous chapter we referred to his vocation. God calls, and man responds in the midst of fear and weakness. In one of the meditations of a retreat preached to priests, Bergoglio expressed this through examples in Sacred Scripture of people called by God who felt themselves incapable of doing what he called them to do, but whom God confirmed in his grace and mercy. It's worth transcribing the lengthy passage:

> Revelation has preserved for us, for our consolation, the special relationship established

between God and those to whom he entrusts a mission: Moses, Isaiah, Jeremiah, Joseph, John the Baptist . . . All of them felt the poverty of their abilities in the face of God's request: "Who am I that I should go to Pharaoh, and bring the sons of Israel out of Egypt?" (Ex 3:11); "Woe is me! For I am lost; for I am a man of unclean lips" (Is 6:5); "Ah, Lord God! Behold, I do not know how to speak, for I am only a youth" (Jer 1:6); "I need to be baptized by you, and do you come to me?" (Mt 3:14); "Joseph . . . resolved to send her away quietly" (Mt 1:19). This is the initial resistance, the inability to understand the greatness of the call, the fear of the mission. This is a sign of good spirit, above all if one doesn't stop there but allows God's power to be poured out upon that weakness and give it solidity. "[God] said, 'But I will be with you; and this shall be the sign for you, that I have sent you: when you have brought forth the people out of Egypt, you shall serve God upon this mountain'" (Ex 3:12); "And he touched my mouth, and said: 'Behold, this has touched your lips; your guilt is taken away, and your sin forgiven'" (Is 6:7); "Do not say, 'I am only a youth'; for to all to whom I send you you shall go, and whatever I command you you shall speak. Be not afraid of them, for I am with you to deliver you, says the Lord.' " (Jer 1:7–8); "Let it be so now; for thus it is fitting for us to

fulfill all righteousness" (Mt 3:15); "Joseph, son
of David, do not fear to take Mary as your wife,
because that which is conceived in her is of the
Holy Spirit" (Mt 1:20). (*Mente abierta*, p. 36)

God will give us everything we need to fulfill our
mission, but he is not like an employer giving tools
to an underling to do his job; rather, he gives us his
own Spirit.

The mission is based on Christ's call to follow
him to the point of identifying with him. The central-
ity of Christ in the Christian's life passes necessarily
by way of the Cross, which is, as the cardinal pointed
out, the a priori of every Christian attitude.

Contemplating Christ on the cross we realize
that we owe him our life because . . . he gave
his life up for ours. . . . We cannot reply to
the generosity of Christ with a conventional and
polite "Thank you very much." . . . (*Mente
abierta*, p. 61)

And the best way we have of giving thanks to Our
Lord for his self-surrender is the Eucharist.

Identification with Christ implies belonging to
the Church established by him. Commenting on the
words of the first letter of St. John: "For whatever is
born of God overcomes the world; and this is the victory that overcomes the world, our faith" (1 Jn 5:4),
the cardinal affirms that we have to

find ourselves with the faith of our fathers, which is liberating in itself without the need of any additions or qualifications. . . . And faith is something we have to ask for. God preserves us from not being clamoring beggars before him and his saints. To deny that the prayer of petition is superior to other prayers is a refined type of pride. Only when we are "moochers" do we recognize that we are creatures. (*Mente abierta*, p. 29)

Therefore the cardinal asks priests to study a "pious theology," which will reinforce one's belonging to the Church founded by Christ.

We need a faith like the cardinal's, nourished by reflection on the Word of God and the tradition of the Church. His meditations, preached in various spiritual exercises and later published in books, immediately convey the impression of his familiarity with Sacred Scripture, both the Old and the New Testaments. This is the basis of his preaching. He frequently uses the Ignatian method of "composition of place" to help situate oneself in the scene of the Gospel and to challenge his listeners. He also cites the Fathers of the Church and the saints abundantly—especially St. Ignatius Loyola and St. Teresa of Jesus. And there is no lack of references to the Magisterium. A special favorite is Paul VI's Apostolic Exhortation *Evangelii nuntiandi*.

The Priority
of the Supernatural Means

In his preaching there continually appears what he calls "apostolic fervor": the need to flee the mentality of the bureaucratic functionary and go out to meet souls. We will deal with this subject in the next chapter. But he insists on the need to be founded on the firm rock of Christ in order to bring God to our brothers and sisters: from the contemplation of Christ, the adoration of Christ, reaching to the most distant precincts of the world. We could speak, in the words of Maritain—one of the authors read by the Pope—of the primacy of the spiritual in the attainment of fruitful apostolic action.

From this awareness of the absolute need for the use of supernatural means arises his continual request for prayers for himself. He asked for prayers on March 13 in his first words to the Roman people. In Buenos Aires his habitual way of saying goodbye to anyone was: "Pray for me."

I have three letters he sent me in recent years. Whenever I sent him anything, he would respond in writing, in his own hand. The format was always the same: a large card with an image of *La Virgen Desatanudos* (Our Lady Undoer of Knots), a title originating in Augsburg, Germany (*Maria Knotenlöserin*) that he had made known in Buenos Aires. (The image is found in a neighborhood church in Augsburg and enjoys widespread devotion.) In the blank space he writes in small letters, much like Benedict XVI, a few personal and affectionate lines. Here are some: "I wish you a holy and happy Christmas. May Jesus bless you and Our Lady take care of you. And, please, I ask that you pray and have others pray for me"; "I ask you please to pray for me. May Jesus bless you and the Blessed Virgin watch over you. Fraternally . . ."; "Thank you for everything. Please continue praying for me. May Jesus bless you and the Blessed Virgin watch over you. Fraternally . . ." Then comes his signature, in letters even tinier than the already small main text.

These notecards were always accompanied by two holy pictures: one of St. Joseph and the other of St. Thérèse of the Child Jesus, saints to whom he had great devotion, as could be seen from the beginning of his pontificate. On the back of the picture of St. Thérèse is the "Prayer asking for a rose":

> Oh, Thérèse of the Child Jesus, please take a rose from the celestial gardens and send it to me as a message of love. Little Flower of Jesus, ask God today to grant me the graces that I now place with confidence in your hands (ask for the favor).
>
> Little Thérèse, help me always to grow, as you did, in the great Love that God has for me, so that I can imitate your little way each day. Amen.

In the audience he granted to President Cristina Kirchner, Pope Francis presented her with a white rose of St. Thérèse. In his bedroom in the curia of Buenos Aires, he had a statue of the saint with a vase filled with white roses.

On the back of the picture of St. Joseph is the famous text of St. Teresa of Jesus about the efficacy of devotion to the Holy Patriarch. On various occasions when, having spoken with him, I asked for his blessing, he always invoked these saints and in addition placed me under the protection of St. Josemaría.

If habitual and confident recourse to the saints is one of the marks of his faith, devotion to the Mother of God is even more one. His whole spiritual life is saturated with a profound Marian devotion. This was evident from his visits to the image of the *Salus Populi Romani* on the day following his election and to the Grotto of Lourdes in the Vatican Gardens a few days later. He advises us to turn to her, leaving "at her feet the temptations that invade us" (*Mente abierta*, p. 81).

3.

Going Out to the Periphery of Life

DISCIPLES OF THE MASTER

The a priori premise of the Christian attitude, says Cardinal Bergoglio, is identification with Christ on the Cross. When thinking about the apostolic mission, we cannot get around this apriority.

> The Christian mission, which we receive from Christ Our Lord, is not conceivable outside of the context of the cross. Forgetting this fact makes us triumphalists. The triumphalist attitude is not always obvious; it usually appears "as an angel of light" in the choice of our pastoral methods, but it can always be reduced to the invitation to come down from the cross. . . . By contrast, one who participates in the cross does not have to validate his activity with triumphalism, for

he knows that the cross itself is a triumph and therefore our only hope: *salve Crux, spes unica!* (*Mente abierta,* pp. 56–57)

Apostolic fervor is something Christ himself communicates to us when we are grounded in him. This unity of the disciples with the Master makes them bearers of God. But the disciple has to do more than merely carry a message: he must make it the life of his life.

The epiphany of God, accepted in us, takes on flesh in the life of the disciple, in such a way that it can only be transmitted through that "incarnation," that is to say, not by words of flesh and blood, not by human wisdom, but by the scandal, the necessity of the cross: it can only be transmitted by the *martyrion,* that is to say, the *testimony.*[1]

To bear witness is to promote the glory and praise of the Father, by means of the joy aroused in souls by the proclamation of the gospel. It is the light that illuminates the darkness. For that, "the life of the disciple has to be irreproachable . . . It must decrease so that he may increase" (*Religiosidad popular,* pp. 110–111).

---

1. Jorge M. Bergoglio, "*Religiosidad popular como inculturación de la fe en el espíritu de Aparecida,*" in *A la luz de Aparecida,* Archdiocese of Buenos Aires, 2009 (hereafter cited as *Religiosidad popular*), pp. 110–111

GOING OUT TO MEET THE PEOPLE

In an interview published in a book, Cardinal Bergoglio lamented in a more colloquial style the lack of punch in some preaching because the saving *kerygma* is left aside:

> The Church preaches what it believes is the best for people, that which makes them more fulfilled, happier. But often what results is a degrading reductionism. I'll explain: the important thing in preaching is the announcement of Jesus Christ, which in theology is called *kerygma.* In sum: that Jesus Christ is God, that he became man to save us, that he lived in the world like any one of us, suffered, died, was buried, and rose. That is the *kerygma,* the announcement of Christ, which provokes wonder, leads to contemplation and belief. (*The Jesuit*, p. 88)

We have a divine treasure that at times we don't know how to communicate. Seeing with merely human eyes, we find the de-Christianization of society to be an overwhelming, saddening reality. Far from standing pat in a "realistic" attitude, Cardinal Bergoglio holds that we have to go out to meet people. He explains in a very graphic way that today the situation described in the gospel image of the Good Shepherd has changed. Instead of leaving the ninety-nine sheep in the pen to go in search of the lost one, we now have one sheep in the pen and must go out in search of the ninety-nine, who have left it or never were in it. To focus on the one sheep and ignore the others, who in their hearts are waiting for us, would mean becoming a self-referential Church closed in on itself, instead of being faithful to Our Lord's command to go out to the ends of the earth preaching the gospel.

In a pastoral directive for administration of the Sacrament of Baptism given by the Archdiocese of Buenos Aires in 2010, these longings of the cardinal were clearly expressed:

> The Church, having come from an epoch where the cultural model favored it, became accustomed to having our wares on offer, open to whoever might come, for those who would seek us out. (*The Jesuit*, pp. 77–78)

We cannot wait passively for our "clients" to come to us, and we cannot expect them to come to institutional structures in which they don't feel at home. We need to shift from being "administrators" of the faith to "transmitters" of it.

Rethinking pastoral structures is important, but even more important is making all of the faithful conscious of their participation in the apostolic mission. By virtue of baptism, every Christian is called to do apostolate.

The cardinal has given special attention to priests. One might say this was his first pastoral option. By his paternal care he strengthened some priests who were wavering, and his total availability for the care of any priest who needed his attention was well known. He had a phone line that was always open for his priests.

But this priority was far from being an attempt to clericalize the mission. He cautions, too, against underestimating the grace given to the laity simply by their baptism:

> There comes to mind those Christian communities in Japan that were without priests for more than two hundred years. When the missionaries returned they found everyone baptized, catechized, and validly married in the Church. They found, too, that all of those who died had had a Catholic funeral. The faith had remained intact through the gifts of grace that rejoiced the lives of the laity. (*The Jesuit*, p. 77)

In a 2009 article on Aparecida, he urges that the laity not remain in the "intra-ecclesial milieu."

> The laity must stop being "sacristy Christians" in each of their parishes and should take on their commitment in the construction of political, economic, professional, cultural, and environmental society. (*Religiosidad popular*, p. 9)

Each year, Cardinal Bergoglio addressed a message to the catechists of the Buenos Aires Archdiocese: a call to keep their gaze fixed on Our Lord to be able to announce him convincingly. At the same time, the invitation, repeated over and over again, was to go out to meet the people.

> We have to get out of our shells and tell them that Jesus lives, and that Jesus lives for him and for her, and to say it with joy . . . although at times one might appear a little bit crazy. The message of the Gospel is madness, St. Paul says. Our lifetime is not going to be enough to surrender ourselves and announce that Jesus is restoring life. We have to go and sow hope; we have to go out into the streets. We have to go out to seek.[2]

This "going out into the streets" is not meant in a haphazard, activist sense. It needs to be rooted in the Blessed Sacrament: in adoration of the Eucharist. Having experienced the encounter with Christ in contemplation, the catechist is equipped to go and tell what he has seen (see 1 John 1).

EVANGELIZING THE PERIPHERY

Cardinal Bergoglio's pastoral projects in his diocese were multiple. The best known of these were centered

---

2. Bergoglio, *El verdadero poder es el servicio* (Buenos Aires: Claretiana, 2013) (hereafter cited as *El verdadero poder*), pp. 10–11.

on the evangelization of the poorest neighborhoods of Buenos Aires, the so-called *villas miserias* (shanty-towns), the local version of the perhaps better-known *favelas* of Brazil. Buenos Aires' attraction for people of limited resources, from the poorest provinces and especially the neighboring countries of Paraguay and Bolivia, created areas of inhuman overcrowding in various parts of the capital. The cardinal encouraged the creation of parishes, pastored by "slum priests," which have carried out prolific apostolic work and anticipate still greater fruit.

In the '70s, with the country's socio-political and ideological situation in a turbulent state, some pastoral projects fell into the confusion of some forms of liberation theology, confounding the gospel message with a partisan political movement. Often moved by good intentions and a great spirit of sacrifice, they mistakenly downplayed religious content, giving priority to the political and social. In contrast to this vision, Bergoglio explained:

> In historical terms, the shantytown priests are a relatively recent phenomenon in Argentina. It probably started some forty years ago and it took root with difficulty because it was new for the hierarchical structure of the Church. It was also the case that it had to be purified from political motivations, because sometimes the religious and the political were improperly united

and that created mistrust. As long as the priests involved in this work were able to better define their belonging to the Church through popular piety, they brought about an attitude of greater closeness and comprehension in the hierarchy. At that time, in any case, the Archbishop of Buenos Aires was accused of preferential treatment toward the priests in the shantytowns.[3]

Bergoglio's shantytown priests are first of all priests. They dress as such, and have developed parish projects of preaching the Word, sacramental catechesis, fortifying popular piety, and so on, which have produced abundant fruit. In this evangelical context, they have promoted educational projects that tend to give the marginalized suitable tools for promoting their dignity, overcoming their material disadvantages, and fleeing the temptation of drugs and delinquency. They have also initiated, at the cardinal's request, a center for the formation of seminarians from the shantytowns.

With regard to the "shantytowns," in our meetings in Buenos Aires I spoke on various occasions with the cardinal about an educational work that some faithful of Opus Dei, together with many other people, are promoting in the Barracas district close

---

3. Jorge M. Bergoglio and Abraham Skorka, *On Heaven and Earth* (New York: Image, 2013), pp. 165, 174–175 (hereafter cited as *On Heaven and Earth*).

to one of the city's most populous slums. This is a
school for girls, with 700 pupils. About half come
from the shantytown. The cardinal visited the school,
always encouraging everyone to continue the effort,
and he was happy to hear that we were beginning
a school for boys. The chaplain of the school col-
laborates with one of the parishes led by the well-
known "shantytown priests," and one day Bishop
Bergoglio remarked to me that this priest knew by
name the people they met as they walked through
the shantytown.

Among the disadvantaged, Bergoglio gave special attention to the children. In his homily during
the youth pilgrimage to the Sanctuary of Luján in
2004, he elaborated on the pilgrimage theme, which
that year was "Mother, help us to care for life." The
descriptions he gave of the poor children in Buenos
Aires were striking. Children and teenagers sleeping
in the street, begging, scavenging through the garbage,
doing odd jobs, taking drugs. And all encouraged by
a media culture that proposes models characterized
by "degradation and sexual frivolity, devaluation of
the family, promotion of weaknesses artificially made
to look like values, and the exaltation of violence"
(*El verdadero poder*, pp. 140–141). The cardinal concluded this homily strongly:

> "Whoever receives one such child in my name
> receives me" (Mt 18:5); and "See that you do not

despise one of these little ones; for I tell you that in heaven their angels always behold the face of my Father who is in heaven" (Mt 18:10). The Herods of our day have many different faces, but the reality is the same: they murder children; they murder their smile; they murder their hope. . . . [The children] are canon fodder. Let us look with new eyes at those children of our city and be moved to weeping. (*El verdadero poder*, pp. 142–143)

Going to meet people and bringing Christ to the periphery have many expressions. One principal concern of the cardinal was education, also a fruit of his teaching experience. He dedicated many of his reflections to an educational model suitable for forming citizens who will work for the common good of society. Some of his reflections have been published in his books *Educar, elegir la vida* and *Educar: exigencia y pasión*.[4]

In turn he made himself present in these "existential peripheries" marked by suffering—prisons, hospitals, homes for the aged. He celebrated Masses at Constitution Station, a rundown area where prostitution and drugs are rampant.

Bergoglio was a strong defender of life. Every year he celebrated a Mass for mothers and pregnant

---

4. Bergoglio, *Educar, elegir la vida* (Buenos Aires: Claretiana, 2013); *Educar: exigencia y pasión* (Buenos Aires: Claretiana, 2013).

women in the parish of St. Ramón Nonnatus, and in his homilies he placed his *parresía*—a word he used often that refers to preaching filled with fervor and conviction—at the service of the beauty of life, confronting the different manifestations of the culture of death. In addition, he stated repeatedly that

> the moral problem with abortion is of a prereligious nature because the genetic code of the person is present at the moment of conception. There is already a human being. I separate the issue of abortion from any religious concept. It is a scientific problem. To not allow further progress in the development of a being that already has the entire genetic code of a human being is not ethical. The right to life is the first human right. Abortion is killing someone who cannot defend himself. (*On Heaven and Earth*, p. 107)

With equal strength he defended the family against the—unfortunately successful—attempt to legalize so-called "marriage equality." In a famous letter to the cloistered religious of Buenos Aires, he called for prayer to stop the attempt to destroy the family, which he attributed to the evil one. "Marriage" between persons of the same sex—always safeguarding the cardinal's respect for each, no matter what their condition or beliefs—is considered by Bergoglio an "'anthropologic regression,' a weakening of the institution that is thousands of years old and that was forged according to nature and anthropology" (*On Heaven and Earth*, p. 116). Once more, this is a matter of a problem which is not specifically religious, although religion has much to say about it, but it is fundamentally a question of anthropology.

In a meeting with politicians and legislators of Latin America, Bergoglio cited sections 46 and 63 of Bl. John Paul II's Apostolic Exhortation *Ecclesia in America*, strongly denouncing the culture of death and the threats against the family. The cardinal commented:

> We are like Peter that night on the lake: on the one hand, the presence of Our Lord encourages us to confront the waves of these challenges; on the other hand, the environment of self-sufficiency and petulance, pure pride, which this culture of death is creating, threatens us, and we fear we are sinking. . . . Our Lord is there: we believe this with the certainty that the strength of the Holy Spirit gives us. And defying the Lord is the snuffed-out cry of so many children waiting to be born: that daily genocide, silent and protected; also the cry of those who died abandoned who ask for a caress of tenderness which this culture of death does not know how to give; and also that multitude of families in tatters due to the designs of consumerism and

materialism. . . . We call out like Peter when he began to sink: "Lord, save me" (Mt 14:30), and we reach out our hand to cling to the only One who can give true sense to our walking in the midst of the waves. (*El verdadero poder*, p. 270)

There is another kind of poverty, he says in an address to the Holy See's diplomatic corps, which is not material but spiritual: what his "much-beloved predecessor, Benedict XVI, called the 'dictatorship of relativism,' which makes everyone his own criterion and endangers the coexistence of peoples." (March 22, 2013)

⁕

Among the pastoral resources that he used in his archdiocese to strengthen the faith of the Buenos Aireans, popular piety had a privileged place. This subject deserves its own chapter.

4.

Remembering

Remembering God's Mercies

A recurring theme in Cardinal Bergoglio's thought prior to his election to the See of Peter was the need to remember in order to understand the present and plan for the future. This has first of all a theological meaning. In the Old Testament there are many passages in which the Israelites are encouraged to remember God's mercy with his people. The cardinal wrote:

> No one is capable of understanding anything if he cannot remember rightly, if his memory fails. But . . . take care not to forget the things you have seen with your own eyes, nor let them depart from your heart for a single instant. Teach them to your children and your grandchildren (see Dt 4:9). Our God is jealous of our memory of him, so jealous that—at the least sign of repentance—he grows merciful: he does not

forget the covenant that he swore to our fathers
(see Dt 4:31). (*Mente abierta*, pp. 89–90)

His mercies reach a climax with the Passion and
death of Jesus Christ, which we not only recall but
also relive in the Eucharist and in our lives. For Bergoglio, the memory of the Church

is the Passion of Our Lord. One of the antiphons
of Corpus Christi, composed by St. Thomas,
speaks to us of this: *recolitur memoria passionis
eius.* The Eucharist is the memory of the Passion
of Our Lord. There is the triumph. Forgetting
this truth has at times made the Church appear
triumphalistic, but the Resurrection cannot be
understood without the cross. The history of
the world is found in the cross: grace and sin,
mercy and repentance, the good and the evil,
time and eternity. (*Mente abierta*, p. 89)

In the light of these mysteries—the cardinal
encourages us—we should go over our lives to dis-
cover the presence of God in them, and to plan the
future in harmony with his plans for each one of us.
In one meditation he cites St. Ignatius of Loyola, who
asked us "to bring to memory the benefits received
from creation, redemption and particular gifts, pon-
dering with great affection how much God Our Lord
has done for me" (*Ejercicios espirituales*, 234). Bergoglio considered that this text

wants to go beyond mere gratitude for all we
have received; it wants to teach us to have more
love; it wants to confirm us in the path we have
begun, and this is done by memory. (*Mente abierta*, p. 86)

We remember the good that God has done for
humankind, for the Church, and for each of us personally. But we all form part of a people: we also have
to remember the road traveled by them, to be thankful for the sacrifices made, to purify the dross that
every historical process leaves behind, and to look
toward the future, remaining creatively faithful in
our cultural identity. A former professor of literature
and a tireless reader, Cardinal Bergoglio liked to use
examples from the classics to exemplify ideas that are
perhaps more abstract. His preferred image to illustrate how memory of the past influences the present
and projects toward the future was that of Aeneas:
he left Troy carrying his aged father, Anchises, and
leading his son Ascanius by the hand. Aeneas made
his own the past, the tradition and the wisdom of his
ancestors, and transmits it in a creative way to his
son, who would remain faithful to tradition but without a static conservatism closed to innovation.

The subject of popular piety as a manifestation of
deep cultural identity is one of the central hinges of
the Document of Aparecida, fruit of the Fifth General Assembly of the Latin American Bishops. The

present Roman Pontiff participated in that assembly and was president of the committee that wrote the final document. In an article published after Aparecida, addressing precisely this subject, he describes in a long introduction the need for and urgency of evangelization of culture and the inculturation of the gospel. Quotations from John Paul II are so frequent that one might call those introductory pages a gloss of the thought of the Polish Pope.

A FAITH THAT BECOMES CULTURE

According to Cardinal Bergoglio, it was Bl. John Paul II who concretely incorporated the term "inculturation," already mentioned in the Message of the People of God of the Synod of Bishops (October 28, 1977) into the magisterium in his Apostolic Exhortation *Catechesi Tradendae*. The Pope saw inculturation as a consequence of the incarnation of the Son of God.

> All cultures should be assimilated in the Church, purifying or eliminating what is contrary to her spirit, but by that very fact preserving those cultures from all self-destruction. Inculturation is the penetration of the Gospel message into cultures, just as "the Word became flesh and dwelt among us" (Jn 1:14). (*Religiosidad popular*, p. 16)

Following John Paul II, Bergoglio affirms: "It is through culture that the Gospel should approach man, this man who is the principle, means, and end of culture" (*Religiosidad popular*, p. 17). Fruitful evangelical inculturation requires that one know the language, the forms of life, the values and the mental categories of a particular culture.

> Thus we can integrate it into the Christian faith and transform it progressively, until we arrive at a vital incarnation in that culture. Inculturation is, therefore, the process by which faith becomes culture. (*Religiosidad popular*, p. 17)

For its part, the process of inculturation demands three kinds of faithfulness: faithfulness to the historical experience of God in the context of a particular culture, faithfulness to the apostolic tradition, and faithfulness to the universal ecclesial communion.

Bergoglio has cited many times a phrase of John Paul II that evidently made an impression on his soul. The words are familiar: "A faith that does not affect a person's culture is a faith not fully embraced, not entirely thought out, not faithfully lived."[1] Inculturation, he says, is not accomplished by uprooting people: rather, there is

> a constant reciprocity between the evangelization of a people and the inculturation of the Gospel; but for this bond to be fruitful, it is

---

1. John Paul II, *Christifideles laici*, no. 59.

> indispensable to make this culture capable of openly expressing the signs of the faith, while encouraging it to enter into the process of purification from those traditions and forms that are incompatible with the Gospel. (*Religiosidad popular*, p. 18)

Bergoglio never forgets that the inculturation of the gospel reflects the logic of the Incarnation of the Word and is a work of the Holy Spirit. There is an initial model of inculturation in the scene of Pentecost, when everyone heard the good news announced in his own language.

POPULAR PIETY

In this wise listening of God's people, and in the remembrance of God's mercy for his children, one discovers that the Church, which has made its pilgrimage in Latin America, has expressed its faith throughout history principally through popular piety. This is one of the most remarkable elements of Latin American cultural identity. The Puebla Conference affirmed this clearly: In Latin America, popular piety is

> a sapiential manifestation integrating culture and faith: it is a collection of Catholic wisdom; it assimilates in a creative way the divine and the human; it is a Christian humanism that radically affirms the dignity of each person as a child of

God, which establishes a fundamental fraternity, teaches how to see nature and to understand work, provides reasons for joy and humor, even in the midst of a very hard life. For the people it is a principle and an instinct of discernment.[2]

With equal emphasis, Benedict XVI underlined this in his inaugural address in Aparecida, affirming that in popular piety "is seen the soul of the Latin-American peoples,' and that it is "the precious treasure of the Church in Latin America."[3]

There are many peoples and very distinct ideologies throughout the Americas. But from the sixteenth century to the twenty-first, Americans have been spiritually and emotionally accompanied by popular devotions that have opened their souls to transcendence, hope, and joy. One cannot understand Mexico without the Reform or the Revolution, but even less can one understand it without Our Lady of Guadalupe. In a similar way this is true of Our Lord of the Esquipulas in Guatemala, Our Lady of Luján in Argentina, Our Lady of the Angels in Costa Rica or Our Lady of Chiquinquirá in Colombia. Our Lady of Quito guards the Ecuadorian capital from the hill called Panecillo,

2. Document of Puebla, no. 448 (See *Conferencia General del Episcopado Latino Americano, Conferencias Generales. Río de Janeiro. Medellín. Puebla.*) *Santo Domingo: nueva evangelización, promoción humana, cultura cristiana* (Santiago de Chile: Ed. San Pablo, 1993).

3. See Aparecida, *Documento conclusivo*, edited by the Argentinean Bishops Conference, Oficina del Libro, Buenos Aires, 2007.

and the Christ of Corcovado embraces the city of Rio de Janeiro. These are real presences, which have greater influence than other factors in the history and life of our peoples.

As Cardinal Bergoglio writes,

> Popular piety has a deep sense of transcendence and, at the same time, is a real experience of the nearness of God, possesses the capacity to express the faith in a full language that overcomes rationalisms with contemplative features that define one's relationship with nature and with other men; it offers a meaning to work, to feasts, to solidarity, to friendship, to the family and a feeling of joy in one's own dignity, which does not feel itself undermined in spite of the poverty and simplicity in which people find themselves. (*Religiosidad popular*, p. 25)

Reinforcing identity through popular piety is one of the privileged ways to recall who we are. "Piety through its distinctive expressions, which are so lively and significant, can come to the rescue of man, his identity and his vocation to life."

For Bergoglio, the evaluation of popular piety has to proceed from an anthropology that identifies man as "the being of the transcendent, of the sacred." Except for the angels, he is the only creature capable of adoring. Throughout the history of the subcontinent, popular piety has been the effective deposit of the cultural synthesis developed in Latin America, produced in the sixteenth and seventeenth centuries, which jealously guards the variety and interconnection of the Indian, African, and European substrata. (*Religiosidad popular*, p. 23)

Following *Evangelii nuntiandi*, The Directory on Popular Piety and the Liturgy, and some theologians, such as Victor Manuel Fernandez and Lucio Gera, Bergoglio sees in popular piety a sign of the rootedness of the faith in peoples, which "leads to the love of God and mankind, and helps persons and peoples to become conscious of their responsibility in the construction of history and the realization of their own destiny" (*Religiosidad popular*, p. 26).

The expressions of popular piety that the cardinal emphasizes most are the shrine, the pilgrimage, and the feast, which have particular intensity in Marian devotion.

The shrine:

The shrine is, par excellence, the place of the Word, a privileged place of forgiveness, reconciliation, and thanksgiving. In the sanctuary, through the sacraments, the faithful experience the encounter with the one who continually gives, who nourishes with ever-new life, in consolation and hope, all those who come hungry

and thirsty. . . . This fidelity of God is a stimu-
lator of covenants, the "promises" the pilgrim
makes. (*Religiosidad popular*, p. 31)

The pilgrimage:

This is another expression of popular piety
linked to the shrine. It has a profound symbolic
expression that deeply manifests the human
search for meaning and encounter with the
other in the experience of plenitude, that which
transcends us and is beyond all chance, difference, and time. The pilgrimage strengthens the
experience of seeking and openness to the com-
pany of other pilgrims and penetrates the heart
with feelings of profound solidarity. (*Religiosidad popular*, p. 32)

The feast:

"This occupies another important place: it appears as
the closure, fulfillment, gratitude in the form of joy,
singing and dancing" (*Religiosidad popular*, p. 32). It
fosters the unity of the whole community as well as
attracting those outside.

Marian devotion:

This is one of the principal signs of identity. Devotion
to Mary is habitually personalized and singular, and
Mary approaches in a personal and singular way the

people who feel themselves attracted by a statue or picture linked to their community's history.

> The people feel themselves identified with the image of Mary: their parents went there, and they go there today with their problems. . . . The supplication and petitions for favors are a manifestation of the maternal-filial covenant, of an interpersonal relation and a mutual commitment. Although they may be people of little sacramental practice, they respond in the face of sickness or suffering by making a promise. (*Religiosidad popular*, p. 32)

In his pastoral work, Cardinal Bergoglio fostered popular piety in his immense archdiocese. It would take too long to list all his initiatives that evoked a special response in the soul of the people.

Great crowds made pilgrimages to the Shrine of Luján, where the Virgin Patroness of Argentina has been venerated since as far back as 1632, and these events were promoted by the archdiocese's pastor. He always presided and on many occasions spent the night hearing confessions at the shrine. Millions made the pilgrimage every year, many walking more than forty miles from the federal capital to the Villa of Luján. He revived ancient pious customs such as the Stations of the Cross held on Good Friday on the Avenida de Mayo, the main avenue connecting the Casa Rosada (presidential mansion) and the National Congress building. He encouraged devotion to *La Virgen Desatanudos* (Our Lady Undoer of Knots), who, as noted earlier, has been venerated since the eighteenth century in Augsburg, Germany. He gave great prominence to the Corpus Christi procession around the Plaza de Mayo, the historic heart of the city. He distributed thousands of holy cards of St. Joseph and St. Thérèse of Lisieux. And he restored to public veneration many images that had been forgotten in old sacristies.

In the papal audience he granted to the President of Brazil, Dilma Rousseff, he expressed the desire go to the Shrine of Aparecida for a day of recollection.

In his preaching on the occasion of great manifestations of popular piety, we can see the theological basis for the initiatives noted here. As an example, we end this chapter with a homily given at the Shrine of Luján at the end of a pilgrimage made by young people on foot in 1999. Its title is "We need her tender look." The text follows.

> We have heard how Jesus looked at his Mother. From the cross, he looked at her and showed all of us to her and said, "This is your son; these are your children." And Mary, on seeing that look of Jesus, would have recalled when she was a young girl, some thirty years earlier, and she felt that other look which made her sing for

joy: the look of the Father. . . . [H]er gaze is like the continuation of the gaze of the Father who looked at her littleness and made her the Mother of God. Like the gaze of her Son on the cross which made her our mother; and with that gaze she looks upon us today. And today, after a long walk, we have come to this place of rest, because Our Lady's gaze is a place of rest, to tell her about our affairs. . . .

The gaze of Our Lady is a gift; one cannot buy it. It is a gift from her. It is a gift of the Father and a gift of Jesus on the cross. Mother, bestow your gaze on us.

We have come to thank her because her gaze is part of our life stories, which each one of us knows, the hidden story of our lives—that history with its troubles and its joys. And after this long walk, tired out, we find ourselves with her gaze which consoles us, and we tell her: Mother, give us your look, your gaze. . . .

But we are not alone; we are many; we are a people, and Our Lady's gaze helps us to look upon one another in a different way. We learn to live more as brothers and sisters, because our mother is looking at us, to have that look which seeks to rescue, accompany, protect. Let us learn to see ourselves in her motherly eyes.

The gaze of Our Lady helps us to look at those whom we naturally look at less, and who need it more: the most abandoned, the sick, those who don't have anything to live on, the children of the streets, those who don't know Jesus, those who don't know the tenderness of Our Lady, young people who are on the wrong track.

Let's not be afraid to go out and look at our brothers and sisters with that gaze of Our Lady, which unites us. In this way we will go on weaving with our hearts and our gaze that culture of encounter which we need so much, which our country needs so much.

Finally, let's not allow anyone to separate us from the gaze of Our Lady. . . . May my heart of a son or daughter know how to defend itself against the hucksters who make so many false promises; from those who have their gaze avidly fixed on the easy life, on promises that can't be kept. . . . May I never doubt that you are looking at me with that same tenderness as always, and may that gaze help me to look at others in a better way, to find myself with Jesus Christ, to work to be more brotherly, with greater solidarity, in closer contact with others. (*El verdadero poder*, pp. 133–135)

5.

Dialogue

THE CHURCH THAT DIALOGUES: THE EXAMPLE OF BL. JOHN PAUL II

In his address to the members of the Holy See's diplomatic corps, Pope Francis alluded to the etymology of the word *pontiff*: "builder of bridges." He also made reference to his belonging to a family of immigrants, in order to issue a call for dialogue among all peoples and all religions. During his headship of the Archdiocese of Buenos Aires, he received all kinds of people and carried on a tenacious ecumenical and interreligious dialogue. He recalled that Jesus dialogued with everyone, and the Church that he founded had the duty of opening itself to dialogue with the whole world, in order to attain truth.

In 1998 he coordinated the publication of a book entitled *Dialogues between John Paul II and Fidel Castro*, which consisted of a reflection based on the actions and words of the Polish Pope during his historic trip to Cuba. According to Bergoglio, John Paul II,

> from the beginning of his ministry, demonstrated a full disposition to open the Church *to dialogue*, considering it fruitful because, through it, humanity opens itself to the Church in an incessant search for the *truth*. The importance and value of dialogue is rooted, precisely, in the fact that, through its practice, it is possible to arrive at the truth based on the gospel. *Dialogue* is opposed to speaking in a monologue and is subordinated to the spirit in the search for truth.[1]

Dialogue is important not as an end in itself, but because it helps those who dialogue in the search for truth.

Bergoglio's classical education, to which we alluded earlier, is evident in this commentary on Socrates' *Crito*. By way of dialogue, Socrates arrives at "logical truth," though it can reach no higher than that.

If the pagan path, full of noble human values, is fruitful, the Church's path in the dialogue ought to bear even more abundant fruit.

> Christian faith, meanwhile, illuminated by *divine revelation*, has as a direct reference the search

---

1. J. M. Bergoglio (coordinator), *Diálogos entre Juan Pablo II y Fidel Castro* (Buenos Aires: Ciudad Argentina, 1998), p. 10 (hereafter cited as *Diálogos*).

for *truth*, the Gospel. Nevertheless, conscious that the *supernatural meaning of the faith* is not contained exclusively in the consent of the faithful, the Church goes forward in the search for *truth*, following the testimony of Christ himself: in grasping the historical context in which its mission must be developed. (*Diálogos*, pp. 11–12)

This is precisely what Bl. John Paul II did in Cuba.

He transmitted his message, but he also listened: he wanted to hear the people, he wanted to hear Fidel Castro, the workers, the students, the priests and religious, the followers of other religions or of Christianity itself mixed with the practice of religious syncretism. In short, he wanted to hear the *truth* of Cuba, as a way of coming closer and understanding its reality. (*Diálogos*, p. 13)

DIALOGUES WITH A RABBI

Buenos Aires has the largest Jewish community in Latin America and one of the largest in the world. Its members are fully integrated into national life. The whole country was shocked at the deadly bombings at the Israeli Embassy and at the Argentine-Israeli Mutual Association, in 1992 and 1994, which resulted in over a hundred deaths and several hundred injuries.

The cardinal was always attentive to dialogue with the Jews, in full harmony with John Paul II and Benedict XVI. He established a special friendship with Abraham Skorka, the head of the Latin American Rabbinical Seminary, in Argentina an intellectual of recognized prestige. They held private conversations and spoke together on television and, as a product of those meetings, together published a book, *On Heaven and Earth*, that is a model of respectful and open dialogue.

Skorka's words on how they came to meet are enlightening, since they show Bergoglio's personal style.

> I met him at a Te Deum to which I came as representative of the Israelite religion. Before it began, the Archbishop came over to speak with those of different creeds who were invited, and he asked us about our respective soccer teams. It was very characteristic of him; they were the bridges that he extended. What moved me was the thought: "This man wants to extend a bridge towards me." I recall that when we ended, I approached him to tell him something about a verse that he had cited in his homily. He looked me straight in the eye and said: "I think this year we're going to eat crow," in reference to the prospects of our respective soccer teams.[2] I felt that he was really saying: "If you

2. In Argentina the supporters of the rabbi's team are referred to as "*gallinas*," and in Spanish eating "*sopa de gallinas*" (hen soup) is equivalent to the English "eating crow."

want to speak with me, the door is open; we'll speak directly and exchange a few jokes." Every time we met, we talked about soccer. (Interview in *Vida Nueva*, Buenos Aires, April 2013)

Obviously the book deals with subjects more important than soccer: God, prayer, abortion, inter-religious dialogue. But it is pleasant to see how bridges were established on the basis of the trust generated by a solid friendship. In 2012, the Catholic University of Argentina conferred an honorary doctorate on Rabbi Skorka.

Here we shall reproduce the introduction Bergoglio wrote for the book he co-authored with Rabbi Skorka. To understand the meaning of the symbol he uses—the frieze of the Buenos Aires cathedral—some historical background is needed. During the early years of independence, and until the middle of the nineteenth century, there were tensions between Buenos Aires and the interior of the country, basically for economic reasons: the major point of access for goods going in and out of the country was the port of Buenos Aires, which enjoyed most of the benefits of this commerce.

But there were also cultural motives. National unity was not established until 1853, when the Constitution that is still in force today was adopted. Even after its promulgation, however, Buenos Aires separated from the Argentine Confederation between 1853 and 1860, proclaiming itself an independent

state. The frieze of the neoclassical cathedral symbol-
izes the reunion of the Argentineans after decades of
struggle and misunderstandings. The cardinal writes:

> Rabbi Abraham Skorka, in one of his earlier writ-
> ings, made reference to the façade of the Met-
> ropolitan Cathedral that depicts the encounter
> between Joseph and his brothers. Decades of mis-
> understandings converge in that embrace. There
> is weeping among them and also an endearing
> question: Is my father still alive? During the times
> of national organization [and upheaval], this was
> the image they proposed, and not without rea-
> son. It represented the longing for a reuniting of
> Argentineans. The scene aims to work to estab-
> lish a "culture of encounter."

Bergoglio speaks candidly of the obstacles to
such a culture, in Argentina and elsewhere, but he
expresses hope that they can be overcome.

> Rabbi Skorka and I have been able to dialogue,
> and it has done us good. I do not remember
> how our dialogue started, but I can remember
> that there were no barriers or reservations. His
> simplicity was without pretense, and this facili-
> tated things. . . .
>
> With Rabbi Skorka I never had to compro-
> mise my Catholic identity, just like he never had
> to with his Jewish identity, and this was not only

out of the respect that we have for each other, but also because of how we understand interreligious dialogue. The challenge consisted in walking the path of respect and affection, walking in the presence of God and trying to be faultless.

This book is a testimony to that path. I consider Rabbi Skorka a brother and friend; and I believe that both of us, through these reflections, never stopped looking with the eyes of our heart at the façade of the Cathedral, so eloquent and promising. (*On Heaven and Earth*, pp. xiii–xvi)

DIALOGUE IN EVANGELIZATION

Let us turn for a moment to Cardinal Bergoglio's analysis of John Paul II's trip to Cuba.

This *dialogue* was nourished, deepened and projected in the person of the Supreme Pontiff John Paul II, through his pilgrimage, not only as a bearer of the Church's message, but as a pilgrim of dialogue. . . .

Also, evangelization through *dialogue* is not an attitude taken up randomly; on the contrary, John Paul II had internalized a rational plan of dialogue as a concerted plan, a method in his pastoral mission. . . .

The Pope not only fulfills the role of a loudspeaker, a transmitter of the word of Christ, but also becomes a receiver of the voice of the world, of human society.

The role of the Church, and especially the Vicar of Christ, is that of liberating, dialoguing, and participating, in order to construct communion between mankind and the Church.

In this way, dialogue understood as a channel of communication between the Church and peoples is established as a fundamental tool for building peace, promoting conversion, and creating fraternity. (*Diálogos entre Juan Pablo II y Fidel Castro*, pp. 10–13)

It is the mission of the Pope—any pope—to open all channels of communication so as to prepare men to accept the gospel, and that can be said of all Christians. In his letter to catechists in 2006, he encouraged them to play their part in God's "pedagogy of salvation . . . knowing how to sound out (as with a stethoscope) the questioning, doubts, sufferings, and hopes of our brothers," acting as true companions and carrying out their mission with unfailing respect (*El verdadero poder*, p. 48).

Gossip, slander, and grumbling, ways of behaving contrary to dialogue, are often the cause of "internal dissension" within the Church. Much energy that could be used for evangelization gets wasted in this way.

He frequently counseled people to refrain from "scalping" one another, using an Argentinean expression for speaking badly of an absent party. He gave this advice with a smile when addressing the Argentineans gathered in the Plaza de Mayo to follow his March 19th Mass of inauguration for his pontificate.

IN SEARCH OF A SOCIETY OF DIALOGUE AND ENCOUNTER

In his analysis of contemporary culture, Cardinal Bergoglio found not only a lack of dialogue but also an absence of interpersonal bonds. Led by the dominant relativism, by consumerism and materialism, and by the imposition of a domineering cultural model that favors efficiency and success, many of our contemporaries live in isolation with no meaning in their lives, like atoms in a society that is only the sum of individual units.

In the annual messages he delivered in the Cathedral of Buenos Aires in the presence of political and religious authorities on May 25—feast of the country and the founding of the Republic—he denounced lack of dialogue, arrogance, and the breakdown of a shared basis for a life of dignity for all citizens. The primary victims, he said, are the excluded, the "superfluous" ones. Reconstruction of the social fabric lies in the "remembering," mentioned earlier. All social actors have a responsibility for reestablishing a climate of brotherhood, concord, and solidarity.

In a talk to a conference on the social teachings of the Church, Cardinal Bergoglio warned of the danger of overemphasizing the individual while ignoring or setting aside the idea of the human person as a being in relation to others.

According to the cardinal, the ideological sources of contemporary individualism include nineteenth-century liberalism, psychological theories that absolutize the subconscious as the determinant of human behavior, and the consumerist individualism of post-war capitalism. This individualism destroys the social fabric by failing to acknowledge a larger reality.

The relational vision of the human person must be restored in order to establish bonds of love, fraternity, solidarity. The cardinal often uses the word "proximity" or "nearness" to refer to these relationships. The individual should be seen as a citizen, an active subject of society. Every citizen has a political vocation—a high form of charity, according to papal documents: "It is a question of the call to and dynamism of goodness, which unfolds in the direction of social friendship."

But being a citizen is not enough. Besides belonging to an organized political and juridical society, the human person is part of a people, with their memory, their failures and successes, their sorrows and their joys. "*Citizenship* is a logical category. *People* is an historical and mythical one." The shaping of a people is a long process, made up of encounters and confrontations, and requires a moral substratum in order to endure.

Bergoglio speaks of an integrating project, excluding no one and applicable to all, by which to overcome the divisions that have marked the history of our country. Situations of exclusion and poverty that cry to heaven, failure to leave room in a "culture of disposability" for children, the sick, and the aged, call for rethinking of what sort of people we want to be. The keys are education and work. The working principles of a project of integration must include "participation, dialogue, consensus, stability of the state's public policy, the definition of a national project."

Bergoglio observes a separation between the people and their leaders, caused by abuse of political power and the widespread corruption of institutions. On the occasion of the bicentennial of independence, he described leaders that every nation worthy of the name needs in this manner:

> Leadership is an art . . . one which can be learned. It is also a science . . . that can be studied. It is work . . . it demands dedication, effort, and tenacity. But more than anything it is a mystery . . . it cannot always be explained by rational logic.
>
> Leadership centered on service is the response to the uncertainty of a country damaged by privilege, by those who use power for their own

benefit, by those who demand incalculable sacrifices while they evade social responsibility and engage in money-laundering with the wealth produced by the efforts of all. . . .

Every leader, to come to be a true leader, must be first of all a witness. This is the example of personal life and the testimony of a life of integrity. It is the authority, the aptitude for progressively interpreting issues to the people, in plain language, and the strategy of accepting the challenge of representing them, of expressing their longings, their sufferings, their vitality, their identity.[3]

A civilization of dialogue that honestly seeks the truth, a culture of encounter that strengthens fraternity and solidarity, seems to be Bergoglio's version of the "civilization of love" proposed by Paul VI and for which Bl. John Paul II and Benedict XVI toiled.

---

3. Bergoglio, *Nosotros como ciudadanos, nosotros como pueblo* (Buenos Aires: Claretiana, 2013).

6.

A Personal Testimony

A man who avoided social renown and the spectacular, Cardinal Bergoglio had three moments of universal impact. The first was during the Synod of Bishops in 2001. Cardinal Egan of New York was the designated secretary of the assembly, but he had to leave because of the September 11 catastrophe in New York. He was replaced by the Argentinean cardinal, who impressed everyone by his capacity to listen attentively and coordinate the Synod's work.

The second moment was the Conclave of 2005. According to journalistic sources, a good number of cardinals voted for Bergoglio. In conversations with him, I was able to confirm his support for Benedict XVI, evident to all, and also his admiration and affection for him. Bergoglio appreciated him particularly for his humility and the richness of his teaching.

The third event that made Bergoglio a focus of international attention was his activity at the assembly of bishops at Aparecida, in 2007.

Although he has become increasingly well known in the world, in the pages that follow I shall share some recollections of my encounters with him. This is not a matter of personal vanity, but for the sake of the light that direct experience sheds on a person's character and talents.

In the year 2000, I met the Archbishop of Buenos Aires, who received me with great friendliness in his austere office in the diocesan headquarters. He gave me all the time I wished, and I was surprised at his friendliness to someone he had never met before. The purpose of my visit was to tell him about the Pontifical University of the Holy Cross, the Roman institution where I was working, and about its new courses of formation.

Later I met him several times in Rome. I recall one time in particular. Bishop Cipriano Calderón Polo, at that time vice president of the Pontifical Commission for Latin America, with whom I had a close friendship, invited me to lunch at his house near the Vatican, saying simply that a few friends would be coming. What was my surprise to find that the "friends" were the cardinals of Buenos Aires, Lima, and Bogotá and the president of the Venezuelan Bishops Conference!

When lunch was over, Cardinal Bergoglio offered to accompany me to the Pontifical University of the Holy Cross, since he was staying nearby at the International House for the Clergy (the same place where he stayed before the conclave that elected him pope, and to which he returned after the Conclave to pay his bill). In the course of a very pleasant conversation, he explained to me of some of his views on the Church in Argentina and told me with a smile, "I'm going to show you the shortest route between the Vatican and your university," which he did by leading me through alleys and passages unknown to me. Later I found out that it really was the shortest route.

I ran into him on other occasions, and he was always friendly, affectionate, and fraternal. But the occasion that deepened our ties and established a friendship based on closer acquaintance was the Fifth General Assembly of the Latin American Bishops in Aparecida, Brazil, from May 13 to 31 in 2007, for which I was appointed a *perito* or adviser by Pope Benedict XVI.

When I arrived at Aparecida, I was told that I would be living in the same hotel as the Argentinean bishops. I had been away from Argentina for twenty-six years, and my relationship with the bishops of my country was sporadic. It was the cardinal who introduced me to his brothers in the episcopate and invited me to join them in their common life. It was a nice, charitable touch, since I did not belong to the Argentinean delegation. I joined them in their meals, excursions, and work. His friendliness touched me. He spoke to me about mutual friends, always in a positive and affectionate way. I recall a detail of perhaps little importance, but which shows his human touch. Our stay at Aparecida coincided with Argentina's national feast day. The diocese of Aparecida always provided us with Brazilian wine at dinner, but on this day the cardinal treated everyone to bottles of Argentinean wine.

The experience of Aparecida was very enriching, and there I was able to observe the great prestige that the Archbishop of Buenos Aires enjoyed among his brothers in the episcopate. By an overwhelming majority he was chosen to chair the committee writing the final document, a key role that required him to work intensely on the elaboration of the text with the help of the other bishops and the *peritos*. He never lost his calm and always coordinated everything with a heartfelt peace. He presided over one of the first concelebrations we had at the shrine, and after his homily there was warm applause, something not repeated during the bishops' assembly.

In the Aparecida documents one finds much of the thought of the man who was to be Pope Francis. Although the final document was a collective work, there is no doubt that the writing committee left its imprint. Some of the pastoral concerns noted in the preceding pages are central in the Aparecida document: the need for a personal encounter with Jesus to be true missionary disciples, the desirability of rethinking pastoral structures in order to be able to go out and meet the people, the radical importance of popular piety—these are some of the most "Bergoglian" elements present here. In the audience he granted to the President of Argentina, he gave her a copy of the final document so that she could "get an idea of what we Latin American pastors think." A careful reading provides much light for a deeper understanding of Pope Francis.[1]

In 2008 I returned to my country after twenty-seven years away. Early one morning, the telephone rang at home. It was Cardinal Bergoglio, asking about the surgery of a bishop who was living in our house. I gave him the information, and our conversation was full of affection and humor. He told me he would like to visit that bishop as soon as he recovered, and we arranged for him to come a few days later. He showed a real concern and interest in his brother bishop. After a period of conversation and a long visit to the chapel, which he praised for its suitability for prayer, I was able to convince him to let me drive him back to the diocesan offices. (As is well known, he always took public transportation.) During the half-hour trip, he spoke with great enthusiasm about the teachings of Benedict XVI and about the country's economic situation, always displaying a supernatural outlook: an interest in earthly vicissitudes but also a transcendent, spiritual viewpoint.

---

1. Cf. Aparecida, Final Document, edited by Bishops Conference of Argentina, "Oficina del Libro," Buenos Aires, 2007.

Conversations with Cardinal Bergoglio during these years in Buenos Aires were always filled with trust, affection, and a sense of humor. Twice a year we got together. At Christmas, the cardinal held an open house at the diocesan offices and greeted everyone who came; I would arrive early in order to be able to speak with him quietly for a while. The other occasion was the Mass in honor of St. Josemaría on June 26, which he regularly celebrated in the cathedral. (I might add that the cardinal had prayed before the mortal remains of St. Josemaría in the Prelatic Church of Our Lady of Peace, in Rome.) I also went to see him about various matters. On one of those occasions, speaking about a movie, he mentioned that many years earlier, on the vigil of Our Lady of Mercy, he had been watching television with other people when an inappropriate program came on. At that moment he promised Our Lady not to watch television anymore. He had kept that promise, and only watched the news when his collaborators told him there was something important. He preferred to get his news by reading the newspapers.

As I mentioned earlier, whenever I sent him anything, he answered with a handwritten letter. I have several notes of his, which I treasure. In one he wrote: "I hope you are over your cold," and in another, an amusing one, he mentioned a letter of mine in which I said that in my last book, on evangelization in America, I cited a text of his. I told him I had mentioned some of his comments on popular piety, first of all because I liked them a lot, and secondly—with the irony proper to Buenos Aireans—because I wanted to "get in good" with him. In his note he said: "As far as the quotations are concerned, there is one step more before they "*cite*" (*citen*) you in the obituaries of *La Nación*," one of the country's major newspapers. In short, the "appointment" (*cita*) that mattered to him was the one with God after death.[2]

The last time I saw him was on the occasion of a reception in the Apostolic Nuncio's residence in Buenos Aires. . . . I arrived fifteen minutes late, and the cardinal, who had arrived punctually, was just leaving. We ran into each other at the door. With great audacity—a product of the confidence that Jorge Bergoglio inspired by his simple and friendly manner—I said jokingly something like "You didn't have to wait for me at the door," to which the cardinal smilingly replied in the same tone with a local expression: "*Sós un caradura*" ("You're shameless").

When I mentioned such incidents in different gatherings in Buenos Aires, others told me about similar experiences they had had in their dealings with the cardinal. I cannot resist sharing three.

A journalist, a very close friend of mine who specialized in religious news, was at a gathering with the cardinal. He asked him to pray for him, since the next

---

2. In Spanish "*citar*" means to quote and "*cita*" means an appointment.

day he was having a biopsy to determine whether he had a serious illness. Months went by, and they met again. The cardinal asked him: "Should I continue praying?" The journalist, who had had a good report from the biopsy, had forgotten why he asked the cardinal to pray for him and replied: "Continue praying for what?" The cardinal had not forgotten.

A doctor friend of mine has three children with celiac disease requiring a gluten-free diet. He participated in a diaconal ordination with them. At the time of communion there were a number of announcements, but nothing about gluten intolerance. When he returned home, the doctor wrote a letter to Cardinal Bergoglio complaining about the failure to provide for these cases. To his surprise, a few days later he received a letter from the cardinal—whom he knew only by sight—apologizing for the oversight and promising not only to take action but to make this known to the other bishops. And so it was: at the next archdiocesan liturgical ceremony, concrete instructions were given regarding Communion for those with celiac disease. This has now been extended throughout the country.

Another friend tells the following story:

> I was waiting for someone at the door of the cathedral at noon. Shortly after I arrived, the cardinal came out dressed as a priest, carrying a briefcase. He began to greet the people begging

there. What caught my attention was that he addressed them all by their first names. He asked them about their families. He asked an older woman if her daughter had given birth. And he asked a younger woman about her children. He told her not to let them out of her sight and not to leave them to the care of their grandmothers, who sometimes allow children to go out on the streets alone. . . . The parishioners entered and left the cathedral but none of them stopped. Everyone looked at us with surprise. . . . I was moved, and for me it was an interior wake-up call, seeing how we should treat everyone.

Here is a heart open to all, a heart to the measure of Christ's heart.

Epilogue for Spaniards and Latin Americans

On March 13, 2013, as I was driving the 400 miles from Buenos Aires to Cordoba, I received a call on my cell phone telling me about the *fumata bianca* from the Vatican chimney. Turning on the radio, I got a Cordoba station that carried national news. I was glad to hear the tone of the reporters: happy at having a new pope, although they didn't yet know who had been elected. The station began to get text messages, emails, calls. All the comments were joyful and grateful to God. One woman said, "I have a hunch it will be an Argentinean." I thought to myself, "That woman is crazy."

After about an hour, I heard the trembling voice of Cardinal Tauran. When he said, in Latin, "Jorge Mario," I couldn't believe it. Many thoughts came to my mind and my heart, for I had spent considerable time with him in Buenos Aires. But I couldn't think much, because the phone was vibrating with calls and messages.

I arrived at Cordoba, where a heavy schedule of pastoral work awaited me. I immediately changed the subject of my meditations and talks, to center everything on love for the Pope, who was, besides, an Argentinean. The climate of fiesta and surprise that filled the country in those days is indescribable, and as I write these pages a climate of growing closeness to the Church is developing. This constitutes a unique opportunity for Catholics: to help our brothers, people of traditional faith but little practice, to return to the fountain of grace.

This book will be published in Spain first. What does the election of a Pope from Hispanic America mean to Spaniards? From the perspective of faith, it makes little difference whether the Roman Pontiff comes from one place or another. But taking into account the logic of the incarnation of the Christian faith, the election of an Argentinean Pope speaks of the maturity of the Church in Latin America, whose roots are in the evangelization carried out by the Spaniards since the end of the fifteenth century.

Pope Francis has a vision of the history of the cultural configuration of Latin America that integrates its various elements. We have already cited some of his writings. Above all, despite so many conflicts and injustices, he sees the Indian, the African, and the Spaniard as united in popular piety. He avoids a Manichean viewpoint and does not forget

that Spaniards were the main defenders of the natu-
ral rights of the Indians and the slaves, along with
being oppressors.[1]

Sadly, there exists in some sectors of Spanish culture a kind of embarrassment about the work carried
out by their ancestors in America. We don't intend
to fall into a golden or rose-colored legend, but we
need not accept the black legend either. To see a son
of the lands evangelized by Spain in Rome can only
give rise to profound gratitude to the Lord of history.
We need to set aside fashionable attitudes, politically
correct but ideological and distorted, regarding a history that, like everything we human creatures do, has
its lights and its shadows. More light than shadow, if
we consider the fruits of the faith in this continent, as
Pope John Paul II pointed out in 1992.

---

1. In his dialogue with Rabbi Skorka, Cardinal Bergoglio notes that
when speaking of the Church's part in the Spanish conquest, one has
to take into consideration that the peoples of the American conti-
nents were not living in peace with one another: the stronger were
ruling over the weaker. There were constant wars. The reality was
that many groups were subjugated by more powerful and developed
ones such as the Incas. We have to look at history in the context of
those times. As soon as we employ an interpretive key drawn from
elsewhere, we disfigure history and fail to comprehend it. Unless
we examine the cultural contexts, our reading will be anachronistic,
out of place. While some point out the abuses of the Spaniards—
since many obviously came for commerce and the gold they found
here—there were others who dedicated themselves to preaching to
and assisting the Indians, such as Father Bartolomé de las Casas, a
defender of the Indians against the abuses of the conquerors. They
confronted customs such as polygamy, human sacrifice, and alcohol-
ism (see *On Heaven and Earth*, pp. 199–201).

As Aparecida's Document invites us, we Latin Americans have to be thankful to God for the great gift of faith, received initially from the hands of others in the sixteenth century, that we have managed to preserve in spite of failures, lukewarmness, and the inconsistencies never lacking in history. Pope Francis belongs to the universal Church. But just as he himself recommends, so I don't doubt that he will "remember" and keep in his mind and heart all of those "brother peoples." Let us take advantage of this providential opportunity to "remember" as well, and to rediscover our profoundly Catholic—"universal"—identity: open to dialogue, accepting of all, especially the most needy, the favorites of God.

I conclude with these reflections from St. Josemaría, which have now taken on a new meaning:

> Our Holy Mother the Church, in a magnificent outpouring of love, is scattering the seed of the Gospel throughout the world; from Rome to the outposts of the earth.
>
> As you help in this work of expansion throughout the whole world, bring those in the outposts to the Pope, so that the earth may be one flock and one Shepherd: one apostolate![2]

---

2. St. Josemaría, *The Forge*, no. 638.

APPENDIX

Letter of Cardinal Jorge Mario Bergoglio, Archbishop of Buenos Aires, July 29, 2007.[1]

My dear brothers and sisters:

The meditation on this Sunday's readings has moved me to write you this letter. I am not sure why, but I felt a strong prompting to do this. At the beginning there was a question: Do I pray? Which was then extended: We priests and consecrated persons of the archdiocese, do we pray? Do we pray enough, as much as we need to? I had to give an answer about myself. On proposing this question to you, my wish is that each of you can also answer from the bottom of your heart.

The quantity and quality of the problems we confront every day spur us on to action: to finding solutions, considering ways and means, building. . . . This fills a great part of the day. We are

---

1. Although this letter was directed to the priests and religious of the archdiocese, its teaching is applicable to all Christians—especially when we take into account what was said earlier about the apostolic mission of the laity deriving from their baptism.

laborers, workers for the kingdom, and we arrive at nightfall tired out by all this activity. I believe that, objectively, we can say that we're not lazy. In the archdiocese people work hard. The succession of demands, the urgency of the services that we have to provide, wears us out, and thus our lives are consumed in the service of Our Lord within the Church. On the other hand we also feel the weight, if not the anxiety, of a pagan civilization that proclaims its principles and its seditious "values" with such impudence and self-assuredness that it shakes our convictions, our apostolic constancy, and even our real and concrete faith in God, living and acting in the midst of human history, in the midst of the Church. At the end of the day, sometimes we can arrive battered, and, without realizing it, there filters into our heart a certain diffuse pessimism that causes us to shield ourselves by retreating into protective quarters, saturated with a psychology of defeat that reduces us to a defensive position. There our soul shrivels up and cowardice shows itself.

And thus, between intense and exhausting apostolic work on the one hand and an aggressively pagan culture on the other, our heart shrinks into this practical impotence which leads us to a minimalist attitude of survival in our attempt to preserve the faith. However, we are not foolish: we realize that something is wrong with this setup, that the horizon is getting too close, encircling us, that something has happened so that our apostolic aggressiveness in proclaiming the Kingdom has been fenced in. May it not be that we're trying to do everything alone, and we feel vaguely responsible for providing the needed solutions? We know we can't do it alone.

Here is the question: Are we giving God space? Do I let him have time in my day so that he can act? Or am I so busy doing things myself that I don't remember to let him in? I imagine that poor Abraham was greatly shocked when God told him he was going to destroy Sodom. He certainly thought of his relatives there, but he went further: Wasn't there a possibility of saving those poor people? And the haggling begins. In spite of the holy religious fear inspired by God's presence, Abraham felt responsible. He was not quietly content with making his request. He felt he needed to intercede to salvage the situation; he saw that he had to struggle with God, hand to hand. Now he was not just interested in his relatives but in the whole people . . . and he risked intercession. He involved himself in that hand to hand combat with God. He could have remained with a quiet conscience after his first attempt, enjoying the promise of a son that God had just made to him (Gn 18:9), but he went on and on. Perhaps unconsciously he already felt that that sinful people was like a son to him, I don't know, but he decided to gamble for them. His intercession is courageous even at the risk of irritating the Lord. It's the courage of true intercession.

At various times I have spoken of *parrhesia*, of courage and fervor in our apostolic action. The same attitude has to be present in prayer: pray with *parrhesia* [boldness or freedom, daring]. We cannot remain content with having asked once; Christian intercession requires insistence that knows no bounds. That is how David prayed for his dying son (see 2 Sm 12:15–18); thus Moses prayed for the rebellious people (see Ex 11–14; Nm 4:10–19; Dt 9:18–20), laying aside his comfort and personal advantage and the possibility of becoming the founder of a great nation (see Ex 32:10): he did not change "party"; he did not barter away his people, but instead fought for them to the end.

Our awareness of being chosen by God for consecration or for the ministry should distance us from all indifference, from any comfort or personal interest in the struggle for the sake of that people from which we have been taken and which we have been sent to serve. Like Abraham, we have to haggle for their salvation with true courage. . . . And this will tire us, as the arms of Moses grew tired when he prayed in the midst of the battle (see Ex 17:11–13). Intercession is not for the weak. We do not pray to "fulfill a duty" and feel at ease with our conscience, or to enjoy a merely aesthetic interior harmony. When we pray, we are fighting for our people. Do I pray in this way? Or do I get tired, bored, and try to avoid getting involved in the matter, so that my affairs go along quietly? Am I like Abraham in the courage of intercession or do I end up in that pettiness of Jonah, lamenting a leaky roof and not those men and women who don't know how to distinguish good from evil (see Jon 4:11), victims of a pagan culture?

In the Gospel Jesus is clear: "Ask, and it will be given you; seek, and you will find; knock, and it will be opened to you" (Mt 7:7). So that we would understand it well, he gave us the example of a man ringing his neighbor's bell at midnight so that he would give him three loaves, without caring if he might be considered impolite: he was only interested in getting food for his guest. And if it's being inopportune that bothers us, we can look at that Canaanite woman (Mt 15:21–28) who took the risk of being driven away by the disciples (v. 23) and of being called a "dog," (v. 26) in order to gain what she wanted: her daughter's cure. That woman certainly knew how to struggle courageously in her prayer.

Our Lord promised the certainty of success to this constancy and insistence in prayer: "For every one who asks receives, and he who seeks finds, and to him who knocks it will be opened" (Mt 7:8). And he explained the reason for the success: God is our Father. "What father among you, if his son asks for a fish, will instead of a fish give him a serpent; or if he asks for an egg, will give him a scorpion? If you then, who are evil, know how to give good gifts to your children, how much more will the heavenly

Father give the Holy Spirit to those who ask him!"
(Lk 11:11–13) The promise of Our Lord in return for
confidence and constancy in our prayer goes much
further than we would imagine: in addition to what
we ask, he will give us the Holy Spirit. When Jesus
exhorts us to pray with insistence, he launches us into
the very bosom of the Trinity and, through his sacred
humanity, leads us to the Father and promises us the
Holy Spirit.

Return to the image of Abraham and the city that
he wanted to save. We're aware of the pagan dimen-
sion of our present culture: a view of the cosmos that
weakens our certainties and our faith. We are daily
witnesses of the efforts of the powers of this world
to banish the living God and supplant him with the
idols of fashion. We see how the abundance of life
that the Father offers us in creation and Jesus in the
Redemption is replaced by the aptly named "culture of death." We also note how the image of the
Church is deformed and manipulated by disinforma-
tion, defamation, and slander, and how the sins and
failings of her children are publicized by preference
in the media as proof that she has nothing good to
offer. For the media, holiness is not news; scandal
and sin—on the other hand—this is news. Who can
fight on equal terms with this? Can any of us fool
ourselves into thinking we can accomplish anything
with merely human means, with the armor of Saul?
(See 1 Sm 17:38–39.)Be careful: our struggle is not

against human strength but against the power of darkness (see Eph 6:12). As with Jesus (see Mt 4:10–11), Satan seeks to seduce us, to mislead us, to offer "viable alternatives." We cannot allow ourselves the luxury of being confident or feeling self-sufficient. It's true that we have to dialogue with everyone, but one cannot dialogue with temptation. There we can only take refuge in the power of the Word of God, as did Our Lord in the desert, having recourse to the prayer of petition: the prayer of the child, the poor and the simple; one who, knowing that he is his son, begs help from his Father; the prayer of the humble, the poor who have no resources. The humble have nothing to lose; even more, it was to them that he revealed the way (see Mt 11:25–26). It is well to tell ourselves that this is not the time of the census, of triumph and of harvest, that in our culture the enemy has sown tares among the wheat of the Lord, and both are growing together. It is a time not to get used to this but to stoop down and take up the five stones for David's slingshot (see 1 Sm 17:40). It is the hour of prayer.

To some it may seem that this bishop has turned apocalyptic or been seized by an attack of Manichaeism. I accept the Book of Revelation because it is the book of the daily life of the Church, and every one of our attitudes is shaped to some extent by eschatology. I don't see it as Manichaeism because I am convinced that it is not our job to separate the wheat from the tares (that will be done by the angels on the day of harvest), but we need to recognize them both so that we don't get confused and are able to defend the wheat.

I think of Mary: How did she live those daily contradictions, and how did she pray about them? What passed through her heart when she returned from Ain Karim and the signs of her motherhood were already evident? What was she going to say to Joseph? Or how did she speak with God on the trip from Nazareth to Bethlehem, or on the flight into Egypt, or when Simeon and Anna spontaneously poured out that liturgy of praise, or that day when her son remained in the temple, or at the foot of the cross? In the face of these contradictions and so many others, she prayed, and her heart grew weary in the presence of the Father, asking to be able to read and understand the signs of the times, to be able to care for the wheat. Speaking of this attitude John Paul II said that Mary was overcome by a "particular heaviness of heart" (*Redemptoris mater*, no. 17). This fatigue of prayer has nothing in common with the tiredness and boredom to which I referred earlier.

Thus we can also say that prayer, while it certainly brings us peace and trust, also fatigues the heart. This is the fatigue of one who does not fool himself, who takes charge with maturity of his pastoral responsibility, who knows himself to be a minority in this "evil and adulterous generation" (Mt 16:4), who accepts the need to struggle day after day with God to save his people. We might ask here: Is my heart fatigued by courageous intercession and—at the same time—do I feel in the midst of so much struggle the serene peace of soul of one who moves in friendship with God? Fatigue and peace go together in the heart that prays. "Have I experienced what it means to take seriously and take charge of so many situations of pastoral need and—while I do everything humanly possible to help—intercede for them in prayer? Have I known how to savor the simple experience of being able to cast our concerns upon the Lord (see Ps 55:22) in prayer? How good it would be if we managed to understand and follow St. Paul's advice: "Have no anxiety about anything, but in everything by prayer and supplication with thanksgiving let your requests be made known to God. And the peace of God, which passes all understanding, will keep your hearts and your minds in Christ Jesus" (Phil 4:6–7).

These, more or less, are the things I felt on meditating on the three readings of this Sunday, and I also felt I should share them with you, who are working to care for the faithful people of God. I ask Our Lord that he make us more prayerful, as he was when he lived among us; that he make us insistent beggars before the Father. I ask the Holy Spirit to introduce us into the Mystery of the Living God, to pray in our hearts. We are already assured of victory, as the second reading proclaims. Standing secure in this victory, I ask that we continue to press on (see Heb

10:39) in our apostolic work, penetrating more and more deeply into that familiarity with God that we experience in prayer. I ask that we grow in daring both in action and in prayer. We should be adult men and women in Christ and children in our abandonment. Men and women who work without holding back and at the same time have a heart exhausted in prayer. This is the way Jesus, who called us, wants us. May he grant us the grace of understanding that our apostolic work, our difficulties, our struggles are not merely human things which begin and end within us. It is not a matter of a struggle of ours; it is "God's battle" (2 Chr 20:15); may this move us to give more time to prayer every day. And, please, do not fail to pray for me, because I need it. May Jesus bless you and the Holy Virgin care for you. Affectionately and fraternally,

Cardinal Jorge Mario Bergoglio, SJ
Archbishop of Buenos Aires